BORN AGAIN

WHAT NOW?

Born Again What Now?

ISBN 9798218156305

Published by Victory Life Publishing

PO Box 427

Durant, Oklahoma 74702

CONTENTS

INTRODUCTION

*"...The word is near you, in your mouth and in your heart" (that is, the word of faith which we preach): that if you **confess** with your mouth the Lord Jesus and **believe** in your heart that God has raised Him from the dead, you will be saved."*

Romans 10:8-9 NKJV

This scripture clearly states that because of your faith in Christ and confession that Jesus is Lord, all your sins are forgiven, and you are now saved! So welcome to the family of God! Your eternity has been forever altered and your life changed for good my friend. You are now a Christian! It is important to understand what this means. Becoming a Christian signifies that you are saved by Christ Himself.

Being saved means that you believe that God did raise Jesus from the dead. You believe that Jesus is alive and have confessed Him as Lord. The following verse sums up the salvation message – *"...For* *with the heart one **believes** unto righteousness and with the mouth **confession** is made unto salvation."* (Romans 10:10 NKJV). Your belief in Christ as Lord has made you righteous. True righteousness is obtained through faith in God, instead of trying to earn or deserve it from Him. We cannot do enough or quit enough to earn right standing with God.

Being saved is not just having what I call "fire insurance"—the guarantee that you will miss Hell and go to Heaven. While you will miss what Jesus calls a "devil's Hell, and you will go to Heaven, God has so much more for you in this life. He wants you to experience heaven on Earth as you trust Him and obey His Word out of love and faith. God's plan is for you to go from being a new believer (a convert) to a prosperous and blessed mature Christian (a disciple).

What happens after confessing Jesus as Lord? What is the next step? Now that you've committed your life to Christ is there more to this? What do you do now? Where do you go from here? These are just a few of the questions you may be asking. We will explore all of these and others in this book.

Reading this book is just a beginning step in your journey for truth and learning what it means to have a relationship with Jesus, not just a ticket to Heaven. Have fun and enjoy exploring God's promises to you as a believer!

Chapter 1

MY TESTIMONY

The spring of 1965 was a significant time in my life as a boy. My brothers and I had the privilege of staying at a pastor's home while my baby sister was being born. From the beginning, even as a child, I sensed something very different about this precious couple. Reverend and Mrs. Woody welcomed us into their home and were willing to care for us even though my family did not attend church regularly. They were so full of joy and there was peace and comfort present in their home that I had not experienced before. I wanted that in my life. Please don't misunderstand, I loved my home and family, there was just something special about this Pastor and his wife.

The more I observed and listened, it became apparent that the Woody's had a deep love for a man named Jesus. I was hungry and wanted to learn more. So, Reverend Woody explained the Gospel message to me. I so deeply believed that Jesus was God's Son, that He died on the cross for all my sins, and that He was raised from the dead, that on the following Sunday, I gave my heart to the Lord. I publicly confessed Him as my Lord and Savior. It was an amazing, very real experience that I will never forget. However, because my time with the Woody's ended shortly after that, I did not know what to do next or where to go from there.

We moved from that area, and I went to churches near me, but a relationship with the Lord wasn't taught or emphasized. I did not know how to develop that kind of intimacy with Jesus. My family wasn't serving the Lord, so I had no support or help from there either. I'm not complaining or trying to cast blame on anyone, but rather explaining my struggle. I was a believer, but not a disciple. Because I had no idea how to be a disciplined follower of Christ, I remained an immature believer for fifteen years. My immaturity created a lot of needless pain and disappointment in my walk with the Lord. I needed help and Christian support to grow in the Lord and experience all His blessings and power in my life. I was locked into a cycle of bondage and defeat because I did not know what my "next" was in this newfound life in Christ. It wasn't until I rededicated my life to the Lord in 1980 that I learned how to develop that relationship with Jesus Christ like the Woodys modeled for me as a boy. I learned how to nurture and develop my newfound faith and allow the Holy Spirit to guide me through Scripture to discover who I was as a born-again believer. Learning how to go from a baby believer to a disciple is vital to success in this life. In an effort to illustrate this, let me take you through my journey as a new Christian.

At nine years old I had a hunger and desire to serve the Lord. I knew that He'd placed a call on my life, so I packed a small bag with a few clothes and was literally leaving home seeking God and His plan for my life. That's how strong the desire was. I remember crying, not wanting to leave my family or knowing where to go, and yet, like "Abraham (Abram) of old" (Genesis 12:1-2), I felt the Spirit drawing me.

God told Abram to leave his own country, family, and his father's house. God promised him a land, but it would not be revealed until he had obeyed the voice of God and acted in faith by leaving and starting on his journey. God promised to bless him and make him a blessing. Abram truly walked by faith and not by sight in his journey. Please understand, I am not saying God told me to leave home (especially at 9), I'm saying that I felt Him drawing me to Him for a greater purpose and I was confused.

Undoubtedly, my mom and dad were not pleased with my plan to leave home. When they wanted to know where I was going, all I could say was "I don't know," not understanding what I was experiencing caused confusion and emotional trauma for all of us. My parents did not know the Lord, so they thought I was crazy. The jury may still be out on that assessment (just kidding)!

While they did not understand my hunger and drive, they did allow me to go to church, just not leave home. That was a wise compromise.

By the time I was twelve, I wanted to be in the presence of God every chance I got. I asked my dad if I could go to church somewhere every day. My parents did not understand, and I started to become discouraged. Think about having that kind of hunger and desire yet having no one to help feed that hunger; no one to help me grow in my understanding of God's love for me or His plan to bless me and make me a blessing to others. I had such a hunger for God yet had no one to help me.

At 14 I attended a youth camp and prayed for four straight hours to be baptized in the Holy Spirit. I begged so long and hard that I lost my voice and nearly passed out from lack of energy. There was no one at that camp that taught me how to receive by faith, so I just begged and cried (How sad!). I was so disappointed and discouraged. I really felt like something was wrong with me and that I wasn't good enough to get anything from God.

When I was seventeen, my younger brother was killed in a car accident. It devastated my family. In an effort to comfort us, a well-meaning neighbor told us that God took my brother due to our sin. Instead of comfort, it only caused more confusion and hurt. Once again, I had no one to help me process that loss and pain. It was during that year that I gave up on myself and on seeking God. I honestly believed I was flawed and felt like such a failure and loser as a Christian. However, God never gave up on me, and in May of 1980, I finally had a breakthrough.

I will go into more detail about my breakthrough in the next chapter, so for now, let me wrap up with this:

It took me fifteen years filled with unnecessary disappointments and frustration to finally begin to learn what being a disciple of Christ was all about. My hope is that this book will save you some of that trouble and speed up the process of understanding what it means for you as a new believer to begin this amazing journey with Jesus. There wasn't anyone that helped me with my "what now?" after becoming a believer. Understanding the important next steps after giving my life to Jesus didn't come until 1980. Those 15 years of confusion and pain were unnecessary in my life and most certainly not God's will. However, He has brought beauty out of those ashes, and now I get to be a blessing to others! I truly desire to provide answers to "What now?" for all new believers.

My story is not one of casting blame or condemning others for not being there to help me transition from convert to disciple. I simply want to be there for others to encourage and support them in their journey.

Maybe you have been a Christian for 15 or more years and simply feel locked into immaturity as I did. I pray God can use me and this book to help you progress in your newfound life in Jesus.

Chapter 2

THE NEW BIRTH

God created us all for relationship and fellowship with Him and one another. That fellowship was broken by sin. Jesus paid the price for sin by dying and shedding His blood on the Cross, thus making a way for us to have intimate fellowship with God. Jesus taught us that the first step in seeing God's kingdom (His rule in our life) is with a new birth. In speaking to a high-ranking Pharisee, Jesus teaches of the necessity of being born again to even see God's kingdom (Heaven's realm or Spirit world).

> *Jesus answered and said to him, "Most assuredly, I say to you, unless one is **born again**; he cannot see the kingdom of God." Nicodemus said, to Him, "How can a man be born when he is old? Can he enter a second time into his mother's womb and be born?" Jesus answered, "Most assuredly, I say to you, unless one is born of water and the Spirit, he cannot enter the kingdom of God. That which is born of the flesh is flesh, and that which is **born of the Spirit is spirit**." John 3:3-6 NKJ*

"Born of water" refers to our first, or natural birth, into the world. Being "born of the Spirit" refers to our spiritual birth into the family of God. The first birth is natural, and the second one is supernatural. In asking his question, Nicodemus was thinking naturally. Jesus explains "born again" as the rebirth of our spirit. When we believe in our hearts and confess with our mouths Jesus as our Lord, we are born again by the Spirit of God. We instantly become a new creation in our spirit man.

> *Therefore, if anyone is in Christ, he is a **new creation**; old things have passed away; behold, all things have become new.* 2 Corinthians 5:17 NKJ

The Scriptures reveal man as a triune being, created in the image of a triune God. We serve one God, but He reveals Himself in three separate manifestations: The Father, The Son (Jesus), and The Holy Spirit. In much the same way, we are one person but have three parts to us as human beings: our bodies, our souls (mind, will, and emotions), and our spirits. This truth is revealed in 1 Thessalonians 5:23 (NKJ) – *"Now may the God of peace Himself sanctify you completely; and may your whole **spirit, soul,** and **body** be preserved blameless at the coming of our Lord Jesus Christ."* When we are born again, our bodies do not become new. That happens at the coming of Christ as referred to in the above Scripture. Our souls do not become new, either. That is a life-long process of renewing our minds (Romans 12:2). It is our spirit man that becomes a new creation.

Ezekiel prophesied of this change:

> *Then I will give them one heart, and I will put a **new*** *
> **spirit** within them, and take the stony heart out of their
> flesh, and give them a heart of flesh, that they may walk
> in My statutes and keep My judgments and do them;
> and they shall be My people, and I will be their God*
> Ezekiel 11:19-20 NKJ

In the new birth, God removes our old, hard, stony heart and replaces it with a heart of flesh. This new heart is pliable, open, and submissive to God and His ways. Ezekiel repeats this promise again in a later chapter with a little more explanation:

> *I will give you a **new heart** and put a **new spirit** within
> you; I will take the heart of stone out of your flesh and give
> you a heart of flesh. I will put **My Spirit** within you and
> cause you to walk in My statutes, and you will keep My
> judgements and do them.* Ezekiel 36:26-27 NKJ

Because of a new heart and a new spirit, now we can mature in the ways of God and fulfill His good and perfect will for our lives. Our new spirit and the Holy Spirit empower us to live lives pleasing to God. Jeremiah prophesied of this change as well:

*Then I will give them a **heart to know Me**, that I am the Lord; and they shall be My people, and I will be their God, for they shall return to Me with their **whole heart.***

Jeremiah 24:7 NKJ

We no longer have a divided heart in opposition to God and His Word because it has been replaced by a heart for both. With our new heart, we can love God and His Word, and with the help of the Holy Spirit, desire to obey God with all our heart.

*Behold, the days are coming, says the Lord, when I will make a new covenant with the house of Israel and with the house of Judah ... this is the covenant that I will make with the house of Israel after those days, says the Lord: I will put **My law in their minds**, and **write it on their hearts**; and I will be their God, and they shall be My people...* Jeremiah 31:31-34 NKJ

Being born again makes you a convert and a member of God's kingdom family. So, what comes next? Well, next God wants us all to become disciples of Jesus. In other words, God wants us to go from immaturity in our new birth, to maturity in our walk with Him.

11

*As newborn babes desire the pure milk of the word, that you may **grow Thereby**, if indeed you have tasted that the Lord is gracious.* I Peter 2:2-3 NKJ

We are like newborn babes when we get saved. Peter was a disciple of Jesus and an early apostle of His church. He said that, as newborn babies, we need to desire the sincere milk of God's word because it will cause us to grow spiritually. Much like good food helps our physical bodies grow and mature, God's word helps us grow in our spiritual understanding and to walk in the ways of the Lord. It causes us to go from being immature in the things of God to a healthy and mature life with Him.

As a believer, we have experienced that the Lord is good by faith. It is by that same faith that we feed on His Word. By doing so we let Him bring about steady change, just as a baby experiences steady growth. Matthew 4:3-4 (NKJ) tells of Jesus' temptation by Satan in the wilderness. Jesus went without food for 40 days—and physical starvation began to set in. *"Now when the tempter came to Him, he said, 'If You are the Son of God, command that these stones become bread.' But He answered and said, 'It is written, Man shall not live by **bread** alone, but by every **word** that proceeds from the mouth of God."*

He used bread and God's Word interchangeably. God's Word is food to our soul and spirit man; like bread, or food, is to our natural man. Just like our bodies cannot grow without food, our souls cannot mature and grow spiritually without a steady diet of God's Word.

Hearing, reading, studying, and learning to meditate on God's Word is necessary for our newfound faith and life. It is the foundation upon which we build our new lives. It is how we grow in our faith.

> *So, then faith comes by hearing, and hearing by the word of God.* Romans 10:17 NKJ

Keep hearing and exalting God's Word and learn to act on it in "faith obedience" and transformational growth will occur.

As I said earlier, I was born again in 1965. My commitment to Christ was sincere. I became a convert but had no help in becoming a disciple. During my childhood and early adult life, my parents searched for God but never made a commitment to Jesus as Lord. (I did have the privilege of leading both to the Lord in their later years). So, because of a lack of teaching and help in becoming a disciple of Jesus, I lived a completely defeated Christian life for 15 years after being born again. I had a hunger for God, but no instruction on how to search the Scriptures, how to pray, walk with God, or how to overcome sin and the world. I did not realize that God's Word would give me the ability to deal with guilt, condemnation, and shame. It would also help me grow spiritually by learning to feed on it.

It wasn't until May of 1980 that the process of maturity became a reality in my life. I had an encounter with God where I had an open vision of the Cross and saw God's love for me in the death, burial, and resurrection of Jesus. I saw the Gospel (good news) of Jesus' love for me in dying for all my sins. I also saw my identity in and with Christ at the Cross. By revelation, I saw how Jesus not only died for me at the Cross but how He died as me. When He died, I died. When He was buried, I was buried. When He was raised from the dead and seated, I was too. He was made sin with my sin so I could be made righteous with His righteousness. That is what this scripture is referring to: "...*For He hath made Him (Jesus) to be sin for us who knew no sin; that we might be made the righteousness of God in Him* (2 Corinthians 5:21, KJV, parenthesis mine). Jesus knew no sin (He did not sin) but was made sin on the cross with my sin. He identified with me at the cross. I, who have known no righteousness (I did not earn or do anything right to be saved), have now been made righteous with the righteousness of Jesus. I am identified with Him and the resurrection.

A new hunger for God came into my heart and I began to search the Scriptures for truth. It was like food to my heart, causing progressive change and victory in my life. I went from being a convert to a disciple. I discovered what being born again was, and how God's salvation worked in my life. (I go into detail concerning this vision in my book "Identity Theft"). I was never taught that I was three distinct, separate parts and that salvation works in each of those parts. What a life changer for me. Let's look at it again more closely:

*Now may the God of peace Himself sanctify you completely; and may your whole **spirit, soul, and body** be preserved blameless at the coming of our Lord Jesus*

Christ. He who calls you is faithful, who also will do it. 1
Thessalonians 5:23-24 NKJ

This Scripture speaks of your three parts: spirit, soul, and body. You are a spirit being, created in God's image and likeness. You have a soul (mind, will, thoughts, intellect, and emotions), and you live in your body. As I was years ago, most people are only aware of two parts: soul and body. The soul is the seat of the personality, thoughts, and emotions – who many think they really are. The body is just that, the physical body. Scripture teaches that your body is simply the house you live in (like a glove is to your hand). However, your heart, which is the combination of your spirit and soul, is the REAL you! *"For the word of God is living and powerful, and sharper than any two-edged sword, piercing even to the division of **soul and spirit**, and of joints and marrow, and is a discerner of the thoughts and intents of the **heart.**"* (Hebrews 4:12 NKJ).

Your spirit is the part that is born again. It is changed completely and made whole by the Holy Spirit; saved and made righteous before God right now and forever. It is perfected forever by the sacrifice Jesus made on the cross: *"Not with the blood of goats and calves, but with his own blood He entered the Most Holy Place once for all, having obtained **eternal redemption.**"* (Hebrews 9:12 NKJ). Your soul is in the process of salvation as your mind is renewed by the Word of God. Your body is decaying while your inward man (soul) is renewed: *Therefore we do not lose heart. Even though our outward man is perishing, yet the inward man is being **renewed day by day.**"*

15

(2 Corinthians 4:16 NKJ). Salvation is at work in all three parts but in different ways. Your spirit is saved (past tense) by the blood of Jesus and His work on the cross: *"For by grace you have been saved through faith..."* (Ephesians 2:8 NKJ). Your soul is being saved (present tense) by the *"washing of the water of the Word"* (Ephesians 5:26 KJV) and your body will be saved at the appearing of Jesus and His kingdom (future tense) *"...even we ourselves groan within ourselves, eagerly waiting for the adoption, the **redemption of our body**."* (Romans 8:23 NKJ).

Ephesians 2:8 uses the phrase *"have been saved"* in the past tense referring to our spirit. Your spirit man has already been saved by faith. It is your spirit that is born again and sealed by the Holy Spirit. It is not corrupted by any sin because it is born of an incorruptible seed: *"having been born again, not of corruptible seed, but incorruptible, through the word of God which lives and abides forever,"* (1 Peter 1:23 NKJ). It remains righteous and truly holy in the sight of God no matter what happens in your mind or body. It is one spirit with the Lord: *"But he who is joined to the Lord is one spirit with Him."* (1 Corinthians 6:17 NKJ) *And do not be conformed to this world, but be transformed by the **renewing of your mind**..."* (Romans 12:2 NKJ).

Your soul is referred to in the present tense. Your soul (mind, will, and emotions) is continually being saved by the Word of God, and your mind is being renewed to God's Word. Being changed from glory to glory and faith to faith.

*"...For we are saved in this **hope**..."* (Romans 8:23-24 NKJ) This is future tense. When Jesus returns, our bodies will be made incorruptible, and we will live eternally with Christ. "For we *walk by faith, not by sight.*" (2 Corinthians 5:7 NKJ). Walking by faith and not by sight means we are trusting the finished work of Christ and our new condition in Him regardless of our unrenewed minds and fallen bodies. While sin may be working in our soul and body, it can never touch our born-again spirit! When we walk by faith and not by sight, we believe God's Word and His work at the Cross on our behalf regardless of feelings, thoughts, or circumstances. Simply put, we believe in God's Word above all things.

As you read, study, and meditate on God's Word, there is a washing of your mind from a secular worldview to a renewed mind with a biblical worldview. Your will, thoughts, desires, and emotions are cleansed and changed by the word of God. Let me be clear, I do not believe in "brain-washing" anyone; however, I do believe your mind needs to be washed by God's Word.

When you believe God raised Jesus from the dead and confess Him as Lord, you are saved: *"that is you confess with your mouth the Lord Jesus and believe in your heart that God has raised Him from the dead, you will be saved. For with the heart one believes unto righteousness, and with the mouth confession is made unto salvation."* (Romans 10:9-10 NKJ). You are forgiven of all your sins and have eternal redemption: *"...but with His own blood He entered the Most Holy Place once for all, having obtained eternal redemption."* (Hebrews 9:12 NKJ). You are secure and heaven is your new residence. The heaven or hell issue is totally and completely resolved. If you are born-again, it is forever! Heaven is now changing your life from within. When or if we sin, we simply repent and receive our forgiveness and the cleansing of our souls and bodies from the effects of sin. As we look to the new life of Christ in our born-again spirit, it dominates our minds and bodies. Holiness is a by-product of the new life of Christ in us.

Romans 6:22 (NKJ) says: *"But now, having become slaves of God, you have your **fruit** to holiness, and the end, everlasting life."* Holiness in our life is not from self-effort or our ability to do good; it is the outworking of the life of Christ in our lives. It is the fruit of the root of Christ in you, the "hope of glory." Now that we are saved (Christ in us) we are being saved from the darkness and death of sin in this world. We are saved now (born-again); we are being saved (from sin/darkness/sickness) as our minds are being renewed to God's amazing grace and love for us in Christ. Our bodies are decaying because of **sin** working in our flesh, but they are saved by hope in the resurrection or return of Jesus. This hope is as certain as Jesus was raised from the dead. I am as sure of our bodies being redeemed (future tense) as I am that Jesus was raised from the dead (past tense).

When Jesus said, *"You must be born again"* (John 3:7 NKJ), He was referring to your spirit, not your body. Remember that Nicodemus asked... *"How can a man be born when he is old? Can he enter a second time into his mother's womb and be born?"* (John 3:4 NKJ). Jesus' response was one of surprise and shock, *"Are you the teacher of Israel and do not know these things?"* (John 3:10 NKJ). That which is flesh is flesh, and that which is spirit is spirit. Nicodemus should have known what Ezekiel and Jeremiah had promised would come in this new covenant. We, too, should know what has happened to us in being born again.

Jesus said that the new birth is the recreation of the human spirit. When you make Jesus Lord, it is your spirit that gets born again. Your soul (mind, will, thoughts, and emotions) must be renewed each day by feeding on God's Word. Your body is decaying and will eventually die. Your body will be buried corruptible but will be raised from the dead incorruptible! If the Lord returns before you die physically, your body will be changed in a moment, in the twinkling of an eye:

In a moment, in the twinkling of an eye, at the last trumpet. For the trumpet will sound, and the dead will be raised incorruptible, and we shall be changed. 1 Corinthians 15:52 NKJ

Then we who are alive and remain shall be caught up together with them in the clouds to meet the Lord in the air, And thus we shall always be with the Lord 1 Thessalonians 4:17 NKJ

Your spirit is the part that has been changed and made righteous in the eyes of God. It has a new condition joined to Christ Himself as stated here – "*But he who is joined to the Lord is one spirit with Him*" (1 Corinthians 6:17 NKJ). When you are born again, your spirit is united with Christ and you are one spirit with Him. As you renew your minds to what God's Word says about your spirit man, your life is transformed day by day.

Chapter 3

NEXT STEPS

A GOOD CHURCH

Now that we have discussed what it means to be born again, let's walk through what happens next. According to God's Word, we are not to forsake assembling together:

> *Let us hold fast the confession of our hope without wavering, for He who promised is faithful. And let us consider one another in order to stir up love and good works, **not forsaking the assembling of ourselves together**, as is the manner of some, but exhorting one another, and so much the more as you see the Day approaching.* Hebrews 10:23-25 NKJ

What the author of the book of Hebrews is talking about is finding a good church. That was the missing piece for me when I was a young believer—a good church with more mature believers to help me grow in my newfound faith. No matter how long we have been walking with the Lord, we will always need more mature believers to help us mature and grow. Based on my experience, that is especially true for new believers. As a new member of God's family, you will need more mature Christians to help you transition from a brand-new Christian into becoming a disciple of Christ. That is why the Scriptures advise us to *"not forsake assembling together"* (Hebrews 10:25).

Also notice we are to provoke one another to *"love and good works"* (Hebrews 10:24). Good works are works of faith that please God. A good church shows us God's love and teaches us how to love one another with His love. God's kind of love is not based on emotions, but instead, it is established in God Himself. It is *"shed abroad in our hearts by the Holy Ghost"* (Romans 5:5 KJV). A good church helps us with our new focus on God's kingdom and worshipping the King of that kingdom. They encourage us to stay in God's Word as we navigate life's challenges. We are taught by the Spirit, God's Word, and one another. God commands us to gather together because we need each other. We need to be taught the things of God and encouraged from time to time. That's what it means to "exhort one another." When we face things in this life that can discourage us, it is important that we are surrounded by believers who can encourage us. All of us need to be taught how to love and receive God's love. We need to be stirred up to do good works with the right motives. I know that I certainly need to be encouraged throughout the challenges of life, especially when I fail. A good church will also help us develop rhythms of grace and faith in our lives.

RHYTHMS OF GRACE

Rhythms of grace are simply great habits to have when transitioning into a disciple. When I say rhythms of grace and faith, I am referring to disciplines that are a part of being a disciple of Christ. It is important to pause here and discuss what grace is and what it is not. Grace is not opposed to disciplines in spiritual matters, but when we use those disciplines to earn or try to deserve something from God, we have stepped out of grace and into legalism. True grace positions us to receive God's provisions and blessings in our lives out of love for God and each other. Grace will never require us to do something out of guilt or condemnation. Its only motivation is love.

An important rhythm of grace is attending a good church. It's not that we **have** to go to church, it's that we **get** to. But what makes a good church? A good church teaches God's word as the "final authority" in our lives and that it maintains loyalty to Jesus. It offers opportunities to be part of a larger community while serving one another. A good church cares about individual and family development and helps us learn how to study the Bible for ourselves. It also teaches us how to grow in grace through a knowledge of God – *"Grace and peace be multiplied to you in the knowledge of God and of Jesus our Lord."* (2 Peter 1:2 KJV) and *"faith comes by hearing and hearing by the word of God"* (Romans 10:17 NKJ).

Other rhythms of grace and faith include prayer, learning to pray, and meditating on God's word (just to mention a few). Remember that grace is God abounding toward us in great love and blessings, faith is us receiving and responding to His goodness.

Because the concept of God's kind of love is foreign to this world and our unrenewed minds, learning God's love for us and how to love others is another major part of the maturing process. The adage "Love is taught, not caught" may be a cliché, but it is true. We need to be taught about God's love for us and how it applies to our daily lives. We also need to be taught about who we are in Christ now that we are part of His kingdom. These are the things I missed after being born again that locked me into a life of failure and defeat. Scripture teaches us that older women have a role in helping the younger women: *"That they may teach the young women to be sober, **to love** their husbands, **to love** their children"* (Titus 2:4 KJV). This is true for older men as well. We are taught to love.

WHY CHURCH

> *"And I also say to you that you are Peter, and on this rock,* ***I will build My church***, *and the gates of Hades shall not prevail against it."* Matthew 16:18 NKJ

Let me clear up any possible confusion before we go any further. When Christ refers to His church in Scripture, He is talking about us, His body of believers, not the physical building. As believers, we are to assemble in buildings, homes, or online as a way to encourage one another and be equipped with teaching to transform our lives. Remember that **we** are the church, the building is not the church. The word church in the Greek language is EKKLESIA (Strongs G1577). It means a calling out, a popular meeting, especially a religious congregation: assembly. A building is a blessing for us to assemble; but **we** are the called-out ones, the Church.

We need a place of love and security where instruction and correction can be experienced in God's love. We need to be taught right from wrong in a place where God's unconditional love is enjoyed and experienced. That place is the Church of the Lord Jesus. In addition to the things I have already shared, let me outline why finding a good church matters:

In the second chapter of Acts, 120 people were filled with the Spirit and Peter preached to the crowd that had gathered for the day of Pentecost. Three thousand repented and were baptized in Jesus' name making the church 3,120 people. They continued steadfastly in four major things that put them on the road to maturity. These are the four major spiritual food groups for becoming a disciple. A balanced diet in these will bring about healthy spiritual growth. What are these four things?

> *"...then they that gladly received His word were baptized:*
> *And the same day there were added unto them (the*
> *120) about three thousand souls. And they continued*

steadfastly in the Apostles doctrine and fellowship and in breaking of bread and in prayers." Acts 2:41-42 KJV

The Apostles Doctrine, Fellowship, Breaking of Bread, and Prayers. These are the four major "food groups" for spiritual growth. We need these four elements for a healthy spiritual life just as we need the four natural food groups for our physical health. The four natural food groups: fruits/vegetables, meats/proteins, dairy, and whole grains, should be eaten in balance for healthy growth. The same is true of the four spiritual food groups. The key to health and growth is a balanced diet of all four groups.

When I first started pastoring in Durant, OK, we had less than a hundred people in a double-wide trailer. One day while in prayer the Lord asked me, "What would you do if I added 3,000 people to your congregation?" The town was only 12,000-15,000 people at that time so I was a little set back by the question and immediately thought that this could not be God. Plus, I knew I was not mature enough to handle 3,000 members right then. (God always calls us to bigger things than ourselves or our surroundings).

After continuing to pray a while longer, I was convinced that God was speaking to me and that I needed to tune my ear to His voice. I have learned that when God asks a question it's not because He does not know the answer! I knew I didn't have the answer, but that God wanted to show me something. He took me to Acts 2:41-42 and revealed to me the four spiritual food groups for healthy growth. I have spent years developing those four and integrating them into rhythms of His grace for our church. By the time I stepped down as the Senior Pastor, we were well over 6,000 members in total. God is *"...able to do exceedingly abundantly above all that we can ask or think according to the power that works in us"*. (Ephesians 3:20 NKJ).

Chapter 4

SPIRITUAL GROWTH TRACK

...And they continued steadfastly in the Apostle's doctrine and fellowship and in breaking of bread and in prayers.

Acts 2:41-42 NKJ

The Apostle's Doctrine – Doctrine simply means teaching. The Apostle's doctrine is the New Testament (New Covenant). The New Testament explains what the Old Testament contains. The New Testament brings substance to all the types and shadows of the old. Both the Old and New Testaments bring transformation from the world's philosophies to God's philosophy. It will transform our minds from a secular worldview to a biblical worldview. A good church exalts God's word above all things.

"All Scripture is given by inspiration of God, and is profitable for doctrine, for reproof, for correction, for instruction in righteousness, that the man of God may be complete, thoroughly equipped for every good work. 2 Timothy 3:16-17 NKJ

The Old Covenant has people, patterns, and principles that apply to today, but it was a temporary covenant to bring us to the new. We must learn God's word (Apostle's doctrine) instead of the world's philosophies. We are not to be conformed to this world but transformed by God's Word (Romans 12:2). While the entire Word of God is necessary to grow and mature, I recommend starting with the New Testament, specifically the book of Matthew, and then move on to the Epistles (letters) written by Paul and the other Apostles to the new churches birthed from the Day of Pentecost. In the last chapter of this book, I will elaborate on our new identity revealed in the Epistles. To grow and mature spiritually, we must get an understanding of New Testament grace versus Old Testament law. We must get a revelation of "who we are in Christ" versus "who we aren't after the flesh." When you make God's word the final authority in your life, transformation, and maturity will transpire.

Fellowship – Humans were created for relationships and fellowship. In fact, in many ways, the quality of our lives is measured by the health of our relationships. God has reconciled us back to Himself through Jesus and the Cross and now we need to be reconciled with each other. The word fellowship in the Greek language is KOINONIA (Strongs G2842) which means participation in social intercourse, communion, or as written here, communication – *"That the communication (KOINONIA) of thy faith may become effectual by the acknowledging of every good thing which is in you in Christ Jesus."* (Philemon 1:6 KJV). Our faith changes things as we share the "good in us in Christ Jesus" versus the "bad around us in this world." As we share what Jesus means to us, and is doing in and through us, our faith is perfected. Fellowshipping with like-minded, Bible-based believers brings about maturity, balance, and growth. Regardless of the size of our churches, small groups are vital to making disciples. This fellowship (social intercourse) is not casual or impersonal. The definition clears that up! It is more than a casual handshake or "how are you?" It is living life together – sharing and caring. After my vision of the cross in May of 1980, God's word came alive to me. I feed on it day and night. Fellowship with other like-minded believers was something I never had before 1980. What a huge difference it made in sharing what Jesus was doing in my life. Hearing how He had worked in others' lives encouraged me beyond measure. What a great food group!

Breaking of Bread – Eating together and sharing in communion builds up our lives. Communion reminds us of what Jesus did for us and means to us. It also reminds us of our connection to each other as the Body of Christ. Remember the "Lord's supper" was a meal as was the original Passover – *"And thus you shall **eat it**: with a belt on your waist, your sandals on your feet, and your staff in your* *hand. So you shall eat it in haste. It is the Lord's Passover."* (Exodus 12:11 NKJ). There are tremendous things that can happen simply over a meal. Eating together and partaking in communion should be special. When someone sits at my table there is more that happens than just hunger being satiated. A meal represents my labor, love, and life. I had to labor to afford and provide the food. I am acting in God's love in sharing what I have. I am exchanging life in that a part of my life was exchanged in working and is represented in the food. *"For indeed Christ, our Passover, was sacrificed for us."* (1 Corinthians 5:7 NKJ). In communion, we remember the labor, love, and life of Jesus. The finished work of the Cross has provided eternal life for you and me. The love of the Father in the sacrifice of Jesus made it all possible and we are now partakers of the very life of Jesus Himself. This is where maturity transpires in a believer's life. *"...And they, continuing daily with one accord in the temple, and **breaking bread** from house to house, did eat their meat with gladness and singleness of heart..."* (Acts 2:46 KJV) There is a measure of social intimacy in sharing a meal, through just food, or communion.

Prayers – Notice that the word is plural: prayers. There are various kinds of prayers for different situations. Many ways to pray that produce different results. I prayed for 15 years as a new convert and if one prayer was answered, I did not know it. Since 1980 I have prayed and only a few seem unanswered—and I am praying without ceasing on those. Something has changed and it is not God. I changed. I learned how to pray. We teach each other these things. *"Now it came to pass, as He was praying in a certain place, when He ceased, that* *one of His disciples said to Him, "Lord, **teach us to pray**, as John also taught his disciples."* (Luke 11:1 NKJ). We all must be taught to pray. Learning to pray and see answers to our prayers not only results in maturity but excitement. A relationship with God who hears, and answers prayers is a game changer! Good churches realize God's house is a house of prayer. Prayer brings heaven to earth and changes people, things, and circumstances to the glory of God. Prayer doesn't change God, but it does change us.

Chapter 5

KEYS TO THE KINGDOM

*"And I also say to you that you are Peter, and on this rock, **I will build My church**, and the gates of Hades shall not prevail against it. And I will give you the **keys of the kingdom** of heaven…"*

Matthew 16:18-19 NKJ

Jesus is building His church. So, if we are going to engage in a relationship with Jesus, we need to be where He is. Jesus is found in His church. If we spend time with Him, then we should naturally get connected to His work. The church is the body of Christ. Just like you are found in your body, Jesus is found in His (us).

"And He (God) put all things under His feet and gave Him to be head over all things to the church, which is His

> *body, the fullness of Him who fills all in all."* Ephesians
> 1:22-23 NKJ

Jesus is the head of His body which is the church, you, and me.
He has entered a partnership with us in His kingdom where we
are given "KEYS." Let us look again at Matthew 16:18-19 (NKJ).
*"...I will build my church, and the gates of Hades shall not prevail
against it. And I will give you the keys of the kingdom of heaven, and
whatever you bind on earth will be bound in heaven, and whatever
you loose on earth will be loosed in heaven."* Jesus promised hell's gates
(authorities) will not prevail but notice we are given keys to bind and
to loose. Keys lock and unlock doors. A major key that the leaders of
good churches must teach is the authority of all believers. We must
bind Satan, or he will illegally and unlawfully steal, kill, and destroy
(John 10:10). I spent 15 years expecting God to bind and loose. God
called us to bind and loose with the authority He has delegated to us.
I was waiting on God to do things that He had called me to do and
then I was blaming Him when it was not done.

We, the church, have the authority to bind things or loose things.
This is one of the many "keys" given to the Church; and is a vital
part of becoming effective in our prayer life. Under Jesus' authority,
we have delegated authority that is very real. We are given keys to the
kingdom of God. In prayer, we can bind what is contrary to God's
will or Word and also loose God's will and promises on the earth.
This is a part of learning how to pray and see results. The church (you
and I) can make a positive difference. As we receive God's blessings in

our lives, we become a blessing in others' lives. The church is to teach every believer their authority and how to exercise that authority. Jesus has the power, and we have the authority to release that power against the powers of darkness.

A key to maturity and spiritual growth is learning to hear God's voice. This is another purpose of being connected to a good church. We learn to develop an "ear to hear" God's voice. While God speaks to us all individually, we learn to discern and process His voice within the safety of the church. God speaks corporately to the church and through tested and approved spiritual leaders. We see this demonstrated through the Apostle John in the book of Revelation. This letter (epistle) was written to the entire church and churches throughout Asia.

*"John, to the **seven churches** which are in Asia: Grace to you and peace from Him who is and who was and who is to come, and from the seven Spirits who are before His throne,"* Revelation 1:4 NKJ

The book of Revelation is written to seven churches. Seven different bodies of believers in different areas of the world. Jesus knew their works, doctrines, things that pleased Him and things that were not pleasing to Him. He gave specific instructions to them as a group. We are not serving a dead God or a silent God. Jesus is alive and desires to communicate with us on a personal level and a corporate level. He speaks to us individually and in our public gatherings (church). These letters were read during services, so it was important to be there to hear them. Many of the Epistles were written to the church. For instance, Corinthians, "To the church at Corinth" (1 Corinthians 1:2); Philippians, "To the church at Philippi" (Philippians 1:1). I am not condemning anyone for not attending church; I am encouraging us all to understand that God wants to speak to us corporately, not just individually. Hearing the truth spoken in love is vital to our growth. A key to kingdom growth and development is the truth spoken in love.

> *"but, speaking **the truth in love**, **may grow up** in all things into Him who is the head—Christ—from whom the whole body, joined and knit together by what every joint supplies, according to the effective working by which every part does its share, **causes growth of the body** for the edifying of itself in love."* Ephesians 4:15-16 NKJ.

Notice it is the growth of the entire body, not just a few individuals. While individual growth is essential; ultimately, it expresses itself and God's plan in the entire body. The church is a living body and there is a supply each of us brings. That supply produces growth for the whole, not just an individual. While our salvation experience is personal, God never intended for it to be private - We need God and each other! Church facilitates growth in every believer's life. We see the power of truth in our lives as disciples: *"Then said Jesus to those Jews which believed on Him, 'If ye continue in my word, then are ye my disciples indeed; and ye shall know the truth, and the truth shall make you free'."* (John 8:31-32 KJV). God's word is truth (John 17:17). Knowing the truth is a vital part of being a disciple. A disciple is a disciplined follower of Jesus. Freedom only comes from knowing the truth of God's word.

Another key to the kingdom and spiritual growth is being assembled.

> *"For as the body is one and has many members, but all the members of that one body, being many, are one body, so also is Christ."* 1 Corinthians 12:12 NKJ

Just like our bodies have distinct parts that are used to do different things, so does the Body of Christ. We all have different gifts that support one another. And just like you have gifts that other people need; others have gifts that would benefit you. That is why this is so important – *"...not forsaking the **assembling** of **ourselves** together..."* (Hebrews 10:25). One of the purposes of the church is to be assembled. It means "a complete collection" (Strongs G1997). We are not the body alone. We are a member of the body of Christ and coming together in corporate worship, hearing of the word, taking communion, and releasing corporate prayers creates an anointing that cannot be done in solitude! In a good church, God is assembling a body to perform His will on earth. Just like buying a product where it says, "some assembly required," so is the church. To be the church God is calling us to be will require "some assembly."

Ephesians 4:16 declares this truth as key to spiritual maturity. It speaks of how Jesus is the Head of the church and from Him; *"from whom the whole body, joined and knit together by what every joint supplies, according to the effective working by which every part does its share, causes **growth** of the body for the edifying of itself in love."* (Ephesians 4:16 NKJ). God's plan is that we all grow together as a body. Our personal growth is directly connected to our corporate growth. We supply one another with necessary spiritual nutrients that facilitate healthy growth and maturity in God's love. This is where we find significance, value, and healthy esteem. Regardless of where God has placed us in the body, all of us are valuable and have honor. No member of your natural body is insignificant. Your toe may not seem as valuable as your ear until you lose it.

> *"And those members of the body which we think to be less honorable, on these we bestow **greater honor**; and our unpresentable parts have **greater modesty**,"* 1 Corinthians 12:23 NKJ.

Every member is vital and important. No one is insignificant. We all have honor as a part of the Lord's body. Regardless of our flesh or the seemingly small role we play in the body, we matter. We may not be on the stage or the main speaker, but we have a crucial role in Jesus' eyes. We may not be able to go on mission trips, but we can send someone. We may not be able to preach, but we can support those who can and buy Bibles for those in need. Every member is important to Jesus and the other members – everyone has honor.

There is an amazing statement made in 1 Corinthians 12:21 (NLT) – *"The eye can never say to the hand, 'I don't need you.' The head can't say to the feet, 'I don't need you."* The eye needs the hand, and the hand needs the eye. The head needs the feet. Who is the head of the body? Jesus. That is amazing that Jesus needs the least among us, the feet. Again, we all have value, significance, and honor. If Jesus needs the feet, then so do I. Jesus needs us by choice. We need each other by revelation. Understanding this is a key to maturing in God's kingdom. Another key is to equip and be equipped.

> *"And He Himself gave some to be apostles, some prophets, some evangelists, and some pastors and teachers, for the* **equipping** *of the saints for the* **work** *of ministry, for the* **edifying** *of the body of Christ."* Ephesians 4:11-12 NKJ

We all have a ministry to unbelievers and to the rest of the body of Christ. The church is where we are taught and trained in carrying out that ministry. Within the body of Christ, there are different ministry gifts that help equip each member for Christian service. For example, pastors teach us how to serve God and others, how to develop our relationship with Jesus, and how to grow in our newfound faith. They feed us a balanced diet to mature and grow. They offer loving, compassionate oversight and protection. Evangelists train us on how to witness to the lost and lead them to Christ. Through prophets, teachers, and apostles we are taught how to pray for others, lay hands on the sick, and minister kingdom principles. We are all taught and then are to teach others. A lot of churches believe the Pastor and Elders are to do all the work of the ministry. No, a key to healthy growth and maturity is being equipped to do the work of the ministry. Maturity will never occur if we are just consumers. We must contribute to the body of Christ for growth to transpire. Church is a place we serve and develop a servant's heart. Where love is not just in theory, but in practical application. Public displays of love and obedience to Jesus are a witness to the world like giving, water baptism, and communion. I mentioned communion earlier in the four major spiritual food groups. Let's look at this a little deeper as a witness to the world.

> *"For I received from the Lord that which I also delivered to you: that the Lord Jesus on the same night in which He was betrayed took bread; and when He had given thanks, He broke it and said, "Take, eat; this is My body which is broken for you; do this in **remembrance of Me**." In the same manner He also took the cup after supper, saying, "This cup is the new covenant in My blood. This do, as often as you drink it, in **remembrance of Me**." For as often as you eat this bread and drink this cup, **you proclaim the Lord's death till He comes**."* I Corinthians 11:23-26 NKJ

The Lord's supper is an act of faith that is a witness to the world. When we receive Communion, we are reminded of the sacrifice that Christ made on the Cross for our freedom. We are a public witness of the death, burial, resurrection, and return of Jesus. In short, the church is designed to be a community of believers, not an individual living detached from the body. Local churches are a microcosm of the global universal community. Church is not just a place you go to, but a family you belong to. We are so glad you are a part of God's family.

Chapter 6

DOCTRINE OF CHRIST

Therefore, leaving the principles of the doctrine (teaching) of Christ, let us go on unto perfection (maturity); not laying again the foundation of repentance from dead works, and of faith toward God, Of the doctrine of baptisms, and of laying on of hands, and of resurrection of the dead, and of eternal judgment.

Hebrews 6:1-2 KJV (parentheses mine)

An understanding of the basic teachings of the Christian faith is essential to the progression from a new believer to a disciple. There are six basic Doctrines of Christ. The word "doctrine" simply means teachings of the Christian faith. These are foundational building blocks to build on to go on to maturity. Many Christians never mature because they never get these basics firmed up in their hearts. Each one of these truths is a book in and of itself. I am simply going to highlight them and then spend some time on baptisms as a "next step" in a new believer's journey with Christ.

REPENTANCE FROM DEAD WORKS

The first basic principle is "repentance from dead works."

> *"And let us consider one another in order to stir up love and **good works**."* Hebrews 10:24 NKJV

> *"Let your light so shine before men, that they may see your **good works** and glorify your Father in heaven."*
> Matthew 5:16 NKJV

God has called us to good works, not dead ones. Dead works can range from legalism and self-righteousness to outright sin and works of the flesh. Both can lock us into immaturity and keep us from growing in Christ.

This is a partial list of what is called "works of the flesh" and are certainly not good works— *"...adultery, fornication, uncleanness, lewdness, idolatry, sorcery, hatred, contentions, jealousies, outbursts of wrath, selfish ambition, dissensions, heresies, envy, murders, drunkenness, revelries, and the like..."* (Galatians 5:19-21 NKJV). He goes on to state that they who practice these things will not inherit

God's kingdom. These are what Jesus died for and has come to set us free from. *"...Walk in the Spirit, and you shall not fulfill the lust of the flesh."* (Galatians 5:16 NKJV). As we pursue the things that please God, He delivers us from these dead works.

"Legalism" and "self-righteousness" are called works of the law. These are also dead works. These are us attempting to serve God out of religious pride. We are striving to earn or deserve something from God like righteousness, healing, prosperity, or blessings. We simply cannot keep God's righteous, holy law in our own ability. It is simply impossible due to the weakness of the flesh. We cannot do enough or quit enough to earn right standing with God. His good works can only come out of our relationship with Jesus, they are a byproduct of His work in and through us.

Sin cannot be overcome solely with willpower or human ability. It begins with an act of our will in repenting. Repentance means "to change our mind and direction." We will never change directions until we change our minds. While we are powerless to stay away from sin on our own, we can overcome it by turning to God. It is God's grace found in Jesus that breaks sin's power. Sin is powerful, but God's grace is even more so. Submitting to God's grace is how we succeed in resisting Satan and forcing him to flee – *"Therefore submit to God. Resist the devil and he will flee from you"* (James 4:7 NKJV). This is what Paul meant when he declares – *"where sin abounded, grace abounded much more."* (Romans 5:20 NKJV). God's grace is the greater power to break sin's power. God's heroic love, forgiveness, and mercy are why He does not forsake us in our weaknesses resulting in sin. It is His presence (grace) that destroys sin's power. He loves us unconditionally and has forgiven us completely. His mercy delivers us. When we fail or fall, we simply confess our sin and change our mind and direction toward God, and He strengthens us. Now we run to Him instead of from Him. He forgives us and cleanses us of all unrighteousness. *"...come boldly to the throne of grace that we might obtain mercy and find grace to help in time of need."* (Hebrews 4:16 NKJV). There is no greater time of need for grace than when we sin, fail, or fall. God's throne is one of grace, not wrath, guilt, or condemnation. Because of the covenant God made with us through the blood of Jesus, He is merciful to our unrighteousness. He promises He will not remember our sins or lawless deeds (Hebrews 8:12 / Hebrews 10:17 NKJV).

Sin is dangerous and Satan uses it to draw us away from God. While we may turn away from God, He never leaves us. He will not participate in sin, but He does not hold it against us or over us. He never stops loving us regardless of our weaknesses. We repent of sin; not to get God to love us or bless us, but to break its power over us. He already proved His love and devotion to us through the Cross and Resurrection. We receive forgiveness of sin to keep Satan from hurting us or others. Sin gives Satan a place in our lives, and he came to *"steal, kill, and destroy"* (John 10:10). While sin ties us to darkness, repentance breaks sin's power over us. When we sin, it creates an unholy alliance with a defeated devil and hurts us and others. Repentance breaks that alliance and its consequences.

Repentance is us acknowledging our need and dependency on God and His love and forgiveness.

Romans 6:22 (NKJV) declares we have been "...*set free from sin, and having become slaves of God, you have your fruit to holiness, and the end, everlasting life.*" Holiness is a fruit of the presence of God in our lives. The only good in our lives is God. Romans 14:23 (KJV) tells us that – "...*whatsoever is not of faith is sin.*" Galatians 3:12 (KJV) says – "...*the law is not of faith.*" He is not saying God's righteous law is sin. God forbid. He said for us to seek and serve God out of it. For us to look to it for righteousness or blessing is not faith, it is the sin of self-righteousness. If we look to our own ability and holiness to be accepted and blessed by God; that is sin (religious pride). God's grace through faith is how we are saved, healed, or blessed.

In John 6:28-29 (NKJV) someone asked Jesus – "...*what shall **we do** that we may work the works of God?*" What rule can we keep to have good works, the works of God? What law can we keep to produce God's works in our lives? – "*Jesus answered and said unto them, this is the work of God, that you **believe on Him** whom He sent.*" Faith in Jesus is the work that delivers us from dead works. To repent is to look unto Jesus, instead of ourselves. We must trust in the finished work of the Cross! Legalism says, "what can I do to get God to bless me?" While grace says, "I am blessed because of who Jesus is and what He has done." Legalism is a dead work; faith in Jesus is a good work:

Do not be carried about with various and strange doctrines. **For it is good that the heart be established by grace**, *not with foods which have not profited those who have been occupied with them.* Hebrews 13:9 NKJV

FAITH TOWARD GOD

"But without faith it is **impossible** *to please Him, for he who comes to God must believe that He is, and that He is a rewarder of those who diligently seek Him."* Hebrews 11:6 NKJV

Notice it is not hard to please God without faith, **it is impossible!** That is why faith in God is the second basic principle. Faith is rooted in knowing and trusting God. Our faith should only be in God, who He is, and what He has done. Our faith should never be in ourselves or others. Faith in God helps us receive what God has provided, accept the things we do not understand, and is necessary for our maturing process. It empowers us to say yes even when logic may say no. Faith is also how we partner in the blessings and promises of God. *"For we walk by faith, not by sight."* (2 Corinthians 5:7 NKJV).

Over time, as we come to know His complete forgiveness, nature, character, love, and compassion, it becomes easier to trust Him. As we watch Him do mighty things in our lives, our faith grows.

Another way to grow our faith is through the study of His Word. God's word brings us a revelation of Him: therefore, faith is a byproduct of the knowledge that comes from listening to sound teaching and reading the word for ourselves. This is what Paul meant when he said – *"...faith comes by hearing and hearing by the word of God"* (Romans 10:17 NKJV).

Jesus said in Matthew 19:26 (NKJV) – *"...with God all things are possible."* Jesus also said in Mark 9:23 (NKJV) to a man seeking deliverance for his son – *"...If you can believe, all things are possible to him who believes."* Faith receives the blessings and provisions of God in all areas of our life. Faith makes the impossibilities we face in this life possible because of eternal life. Faith is how we are justified or made righteous in God's eyes – *"For in it the righteousness of God is revealed from faith to faith; as it is written, "The just shall live by faith."* (Romans 1:17 NKJV). Faith is how we now walk in the blessings and promises of God – *"For we walk by faith, not by sight."* (2 Corinthians 5:7). Faith in God is powerful! If you would like more teaching on faith, I have material available for free that could be immensely helpful to you.

LAYING ON OF HANDS

> *"Then the little children were brought to Him that He might **put His hands** on them and pray...* Matthew 19:13 NKJV

The third principle is the laying on of hands. Jesus laid hands on people. Why? Blessings are transferred through the laying on of hands. Jairus, a ruler of the synagogue, begged Jesus to come and heal his daughter. *"My little daughter lies at the point of death, come and* **lay your hands on her***, that she may be healed, and she will live."* (Mark 5:23 NKJV) Healing is a blessing from God that is transferred through the laying on of hands. This is not magic or mystical, it is an act of faith in God. It is how God works!

Paul laid hands on people to receive the Holy Spirit – *"And when Paul had laid hands on them, the Holy Spirit came upon them, and they spoke with tongues and prophesied."* (Acts 19:6 NKJV), believers lay hands on the sick, and they recover – *"...they will lay hands on the sick, and they will recover."* (Mark 16:18 NKJV). Leaders laid hands on Timothy transferring a gift – *"Do not neglect the gift that is in you, which was given to you by prophecy with the laying on of the hands of the eldership."* (1 Timothy 4:14 NKJV). Moses laid hands on Joshua to transfer leadership – *"...Joshua, the son of Nun, was full of the spirit of Wisdom: for Moses had* **laid his hands upon him***; and the children of Israel hearkened unto him and did as the Lord commanded Moses."* (Deuteronomy 34:9 KJV). Notice how a measure of wisdom was transferred through the laying on of hands. Remarkable things happen when people of faith lay hands on people in faith.

RESURRECTION OF THE DEAD

The fourth principle is the Resurrection of the Dead. No matter what happens here on Earth, every believer has the assurance of the resurrection of their bodies. While our earthly bodies are decaying and will return to dust, they will not remain there. When Christ returns, those who have died in Christ will be resurrected and those who are living will be transformed in the twinkling of an eye.

> *"For the Lord Himself will descend from heaven with a shout, with the voice of an archangel, and with the trumpet of God. And the dead in Christ will rise first. Then we who are alive and remain shall be caught up together with them in the clouds to meet the Lord in the air. And thus we shall always be with the Lord."* 1 Thessalonians 4:16-17 NKJV

> *"Who will transform our lowly body that it may be conformed to His glorious body, according to the working by which He is able even to subdue all things to Himself."* Philippians 3:21 NKJV

It is at that moment that our bodies will be raised with Christ and become a glorious body like His! We will receive our eternal bodies and death will be permanently eradicated!

There will be no more sin, sickness, disease, or handicaps in our resurrected bodies. Praise God! Paul describes how this process of things being sown in one way and raised in another happens. *"So also is the resurrection of the dead. The body is sown in corruption, it is raised in incorruption."* He goes on to say – *"It is sown in dishonor, it is raised in glory, it is sown in weakness, it is raised in power. It is sown a natural body; it is raised a spiritual body."* (1 Corinthians 15:42-44 NKJV)

Paul says it like this – *"So we are always confident, knowing that while **we are at home in the body**, we are absent from the Lord."* (2 Corinthians 5:6 NKJV). When we die, our body will be sown into the earth, but our spirit will be with the Lord. James said – *"For as the body without the spirit is dead, so faith without works (actions) is dead also"* (James 2:26 NKJV). Physical death is when we leave our bodies and go to be with Jesus. At His appearing, Jesus will bring us back with Him and our bodies will be raised from the dead in honor and in power. It will not be a natural body, but a supernatural one. This is a promise of God that gives us great hope; hope in the resurrection where our body will be saved.

ETERNAL JUDGMENT

Another Doctrine of Christ is eternal judgment. Before we really dig into this doctrine, I want to be clear about something. God is loving and merciful, He does not curse us and desires that everyone comes to know Him – *"The Lord is not slack concerning His promise, as*

*some count slackness, but is longsuffering toward us, not willing that
any should perish but that all should come to repentance."* (2 Peter
3:9 NKJV). However, because of man's free will, there is a day of
accountability coming at the appearing of Jesus and His kingdom.
Those of faith will be judged at the judgment seat of Christ and
receive rewards for their faithful obedience.

> *"But why do you judge your brother? Or why do you show
> contempt for your brother? For we shall all stand before
> the **judgment seat of Christ**. For it is written: 'As I live,
> says the LORD, every knee shall bow to Me, and every
> tongue shall confess to God. So then each of us shall give
> **account of himself** to God. Therefore let us not judge
> one another anymore, but rather resolve this, not to put
> a stumbling block or a cause to fall in our brother's way.*
> Romans 14:10-12 NKJV

We will receive rewards for works done in faith and are pleasing to
God. Other works will be purged by fire, and we will suffer loss.
There will be no wrath because Jesus bore that for us at the Cross (1
Corinthians 3:12-15). Faith in Jesus saves us from the wrath to come
(Romans 5:9 / 1 Thessalonians 1:10 / 1 Thessalonians 5:9).

Those of unbelief, those who reject God's love and forgiveness
extended in Jesus, will go before the Great White Throne of
Judgment and God will judge them for their sins committed in
unbelief.

*Then I saw a **great white throne** and Him who sat on it, from whose face the earth and the heaven fled away. And there was found no place for them. And I saw the dead, small and great, standing before God, and books were opened. And another book was opened, which is the Book of Life. And the dead were **judged according to their works**, by the things which were written in the books. The sea gave up the dead who were in it, and Death and Hades delivered up the dead who were in them. And they were **judged**, each one according to his works. Then Death and Hades were cast into the lake of fire. This is the second death. And anyone not found written in the Book of Life was cast into the lake of fire.* Revelation 20:11-15 NKJV

Those who reject God's love and the cross will experience eternal judgment (Hell). Those who accept God's love and believe in Christ have been saved from this judgment:

For when we were still without strength, in due time Christ died for the ungodly. For scarcely for a righteous man will one die; yet perhaps for a good man someone would even dare to die. But God demonstrates His own love toward us, in that while we were still sinners, Christ died for us. Much more then, having now been justified

DUANE SHERIFF

*by His blood, **we shall be saved from wrath through
Him**."*Romans 5:6-9 NKJV

This verse proves how much God loves us. In His Son Jesus, He
gave His life for each of us without any guarantees that we would
choose to live with Him. He wants us to choose Him and be spared
from eternal judgment. While God's judgment to come is absolute
and certain, John 3:16 plainly states the will of the Father regarding
eternal judgment: *"For God so loved the world that He gave His only
begotten Son (Jesus)that whosoever believes in Him should not perish
(judgment) but have everlasting life."* As believers, we have been
redeemed and can be confident that our place with Him is secure. It
is only those who reject the cross and remain in unbelief that will face
eternal judgment. This is the reason we need to share God's love and
trust the Holy Spirit to draw people to Christ. If men reject God's
love and the sacrifice Jesus made, they face eternal judgment. God
wants everyone saved and He has made it possible by sacrificing Jesus
on the Cross to pay the debt for sin.

Acts 17 recounts a story of Paul when he was in Athens and the
entire city had been given over to idols. He began to preach to them
about Jesus and the resurrection. He found them worshipping at
an altar with the inscription "TO THE UNKNOWN GOD" (Acts
17:23). He took that opportunity to teach them who this "unknown
to them" God was. The true and living God is unlike all these idols of
stone, gold, or silver. Paul calls all men to repent of their sins because
– *"...He (God) has appointed a day on which He will judge the world*

in righteousness by the Man whom He has ordained. He has given assurance of this to all by raising Him (Jesus) from the dead." (Acts 17:31 NKJV). This passage goes on to say that some mocked Paul, but others wanted to hear more.

God's judgment to come is very real and sure. We who are of faith are saved from this judgment. We will not face God's eternal wrath because of our faith in Jesus. Jesus bore God's wrath to save us from eternal judgment and grant us eternal life by faith:

> *"...God sent not His Son into the world to condemn the world; but that the world through Him might be saved. He that believeth on Him **is not condemned**; but he that believeth not is **condemned already**, because he hath not believed in the name of the only begotten Son of God. And this is the condemnation, that light is come into the world and men loved darkness rather than light, because their deeds were evil."* John 3:17-19 KJV

If men reject God's love and the sacrifice Jesus made, they face eternal judgment. God wants everyone saved and has made it possible by sacrificing Jesus on the cross to pay the debt for sin.

All we need to do is choose light. To choose light is to accept Jesus and His work at the cross to save us from the darkness. To embrace darkness is to choose to be cast into outer darkness (Matthew 8:12 / 22:13 / 25:30).

BAPTISMS

The final principle is baptisms. There is so much information I want to share with you regarding this doctrine that I have dedicated the entirety of the next chapter to do just that.

Chapter 7

BAPTISMS

The doctrine of baptisms (plural) is one of the six basic principles we have been talking about. There are different baptisms mentioned in Scripture. Some were exclusive to the culture of the people in the Old Testament, others to the New Testament. The baptism of Moses (1 Corinthians 10:1-2) and of John the Baptist (Matthew 3:1-6 / Acts 19:3) were among those of the Old Testament. In the New Testament, three baptisms apply to the new believer in Jesus:

1. The baptism into the body of Christ.

2. The baptism of water.

3. The baptism of the Holy Spirit.

All three are a part of the believer's journey with God. Additionally, all three are different works of God's grace in our lives as we go from being a convert to a disciple. These three have a baptizer, baptizee, and an element into which we are baptized. For clarity's sake, let us start by defining baptism:

Baptize (Greek) baptizo (Strongs 907)

- To immerse

- Submerge

- To make full whelmed (i.e., fully wet)

As you can see, to be baptized is to be immersed, submerged, and made fully whelmed or wet. When we experience any of the three baptisms, we become completely enveloped with whatever we are being baptized into. Now that we know what baptism is, let us look at the three types of baptism in the New Testament:

BAPTIZED INTO THE BODY OF CHRIST – THE CHURCH

In this baptism, the Holy Spirit baptizes the believer into the body of Christ. The Holy Spirit is the baptizer, we (believers) are the baptizee and the body of Christ is the element we are completely immersed into:

Romans 6:3 NKJ – *"...as many of us were **baptized into Christ Jesus** were baptized into His death?"* Notice we were baptized into Jesus.

1 Corinthians 12:13 KJV – *"For by one Spirit (baptizer) are we (baptizee) **all baptized into one body** (element)..."*

Baptizer = Holy Spirit (God – third member of the Godhead)

Baptizee = Us (Believers)

Element = Body of Christ (the church)

> "*There is one body and one Spirit, just as you were called in one hope of your calling; one Lord, one faith, **one baptism**; one God and Father of all, who is above all, and through all and in you all*". Ephesians 4:4-6 NKJ

This baptism gives all those that accept Jesus, one Father, one God, one faith, and one Lord. It is the only baptism that gives us salvation or makes us Christians. A good example of this type of baptism took place on the day that Jesus was crucified. His cross was placed between two thieves. One was defiant and rebellious. He mocked Jesus and His power. The other was convicted of his sin and respectful of who Jesus was. He was repentant and had faith. The believing thief asked Jesus to remember him in His kingdom. Jesus replied that he would be with Him that day in paradise (Luke 23:42-43). Through faith, the believing thief entered into eternal life with Christ.

Once you have experienced the baptism into the body of Christ, your next step is water baptism.

WATER BAPTISM

In this baptism, a believer, church leader, or pastor is the baptizer, we are the baptizee, and water is the element. We are baptized in water by a believer in our faith obedience to our Lord Jesus.

Baptizer = Pastor/Leader

Baptizee = Us (believers)

Element = Water (H2O)

It is important to know that water baptism is not the baptism that saves us. Only the first baptism offers us eternal life with Christ. With that said, the biblical faith that brought us into the family of God has an action that follows *"For as the body without the spirit is dead, so **faith without works is dead** also."* (James 2:26 NKJ). As an example to all of us, Jesus Himself was water baptized in obedience to His Father. Again, water baptism did not save Him but was an act of faith obedience to the Father.

> *"When all the people were baptized, it came to pass that Jesus also was baptized; and while He prayed, the heaven was opened. And the Holy Spirit descended in bodily form like a dove upon Him, and a voice came from heaven which said, "You are My beloved Son; in You I am well pleased."* Luke 3:21-22 NKJ

In Matthew's account of Jesus being water baptized, John was reluctant to do so and felt the need for Jesus to baptize him. But Jesus said *"...Permit it to be so now, for thus it is fitting for us to fulfill all righteousness."* (Matthew 3:15 NKJ). John was the baptizer, Jesus was the baptizee, and water was the element.

Baptism in water is an act of faithful obedience, not of works to be saved. Because I am saved by God's grace, I simply follow Jesus' example in water baptism. It is an outer act of the inner fact that we are a new creation. Our old life in Adam is dead and we are living a new resurrected life in Christ.

In water baptism, we publicly acknowledge our faith in Jesus and that we are walking in newness of life. Jesus was water baptized, showing His submission to the will of His Father. Our water baptism is us submitting to Jesus. We are following Him in the steps to being a disciple.

In our first baptism, we are baptized into the body of Christ. Our old man (spirit man in Adam) is dead and buried. Our new man (born-again spirit in Christ) is united to Jesus, and we are now called a new creation (2 Corinthians 5:17). Water baptism is the physical response to the inner work of the Holy Spirit at the moment of our salvation. We are demonstrating the death and burial of our old man and the resurrection of our new man. When we go down into the water; that is symbolic of the death and burial of the old life. When we come up out of the water; that is symbolic of the new resurrection life in Christ. It is the natural act of a spiritual fact. Now I am dead to my old man and the life of this world, but alive to the new life in Christ, my Lord, and Savior. Again, water baptism does not save us but is an act of faith obedience to following Jesus as a disciple.

Going back to the believing thief, it is important to remember that water baptism was not a requirement for his salvation. I am sure, however, that had the thief not died on a cross, he would have followed the Lord in faith, and water baptism would have been a special moment for him. He became a convert on his cross, but not a disciple.

Now, before we move on, let us recap:

First baptism – The Holy Spirit baptizes us into the body of Christ.

When the Holy Spirit baptizes us into the body of Christ, we become a convert.

Second baptism – A member of the body of Christ baptizes us in water.

Water baptism is a part of being a disciple.

THE BAPTISM OF THE HOLY SPIRIT

In this baptism Jesus is the baptizer, we are the baptizee, and the Holy Spirit is the element.

Baptizer = Jesus (second member of the Godhead)

Baptizee = Us (believers)

Element = Holy Spirit (the third member of the Godhead)

In our first baptism, the Holy Spirit baptizes us into the body of Christ by convicting us of our need for a Savior. Water baptism is our way of outwardly expressing the work that the Holy Spirit does on the inside of us during the first baptism. The third baptism, the baptism in the Holy Spirit, is what comes next.

In the book of Matthew, John the Baptist prophesies of the baptism into the Holy Spirit:

> *I indeed baptize you with water unto repentance, but He (Jesus) who is coming after me is mightier than I, whose sandals I am not worthy to carry. He (Jesus) will baptize you (us) with the Holy Spirit (element) and fire."*
> Matthew 3:11 NKJ

> *And I will pray the Father, and He will give you another Helper, that He may abide with you forever—the Spirit of truth, **whom the world cannot receive** because it neither sees Him nor knows Him; but you know Him, for He dwells with you and will be in you.* John 14:16-17 NKJ

Unbelievers cannot receive the baptism of the Holy Spirit. This baptism, like water baptism, is for believers only. Jesus explains this in John 7:

*"On the last day, that great day of the feast, Jesus stood and cried out, saying, 'If **anyone thirsts**, let him come to Me and drink. He **who believes in Me**, as the Scripture has said, out of his heart will flow rivers of living water.' But this He spoke concerning the Spirit, whom those **believing in Him would receive**; for the Holy Spirit was not yet given, because Jesus was not yet glorified."*
John 7:37-39 NKJ

The thirst Jesus is referring to is not one of physical thirst. He is speaking to those who feel like something is missing in their heart and life, but do not quite know what that is. Have you ever been there? I know I have. In response, Jesus has given a two-part promise here. The first, *"If **anyone** thirsts, let him come to Me and drink,"* is an invitation to unbelievers to come to Jesus. He knows that we have all been created with a longing for a relationship with our Father and that we will never be fully satisfied until we are in a close relationship with Him. That is what Jesus meant when He said that anyone who comes to Him will never be thirsty again (John 4:14). The second part of Jesus' promise in John 7:37-39 is prophesying the coming of the Holy Spirit. This promise is to believers only; *"He who believes in me...."* To those who believe and receive there is a well in them that springs up into everlasting life (John 4:14). They can receive the baptism of the Holy Spirit and rivers of living water pour out of them. The world cannot receive this promise of the Spirit because it is strictly for those who believe in Jesus Christ. At salvation, a well is put in us for eternal life and that well of Christ in us is for our personal thirst. A river is for others and ministry to others. It involves power. Think of it this way, we build electrical power grids and plants by rivers, not wells.

> *"But you shall receive **power** when the Holy Spirit has come upon you; and You shall **be witnesses** to Me in Jerusalem, and in all Judea and Samaria, and to the end of the earth."* Acts 1:8 NKJ

In this scripture, Jesus is telling His disciples to wait for the Holy Spirit to come upon them because the Spirit would give them the power necessary to take the Gospel *"to the end of the earth."* That power would be *"like rivers of living water"* flowing from their hearts.

It is the same for us today. First, we must come to Christ and drink of Him. When we do that, we are given a new heart. With that new heart, we can receive the baptism of the Holy Spirit and experience rivers of living water flowing from it. This baptism is also referred to as being "filled with the Spirit." Like water baptism, this baptism does not save us. Many questions surround this baptism and unfortunately, so does controversy. It does not have to be that way, nor does God want it to be that way. To put it simply, the baptism of the Holy Spirit involves power, prayer, and many gifts available to the church that empowers us to be better witnesses. It opens the door to the gifts of the Spirit—spiritual weapons against Satan, our spiritual enemy. I believe that this is why he opposes this baptism so much. The last thing Satan wants is for you to witness to the world with the power to defeat him at every turn.

> *And you are **witnesses** of these things. Behold, I send the **Promise of My Father** upon you; but tarry in the city of Jerusalem until you are endued with power from on high* Luke 24:48-49 NKJ

The "gift of the Holy Spirit" will be explained in detail in the next chapter.

Chapter 8

THE GIFT OF THE HOLY SPIRIT

In some circles, the Holy Spirit and His power are mocked and/or dismissed. That should not be! The Holy Spirit was meant to be a gift from the Father to us. Jesus calls the Holy Spirit "The Promise of the Father." He also referred to the Holy Spirit as a gift in Luke's account, comparing the good gifts we give our children, to the Father giving us the Holy Spirit when asked for:

> *If you then, being evil, know how to give **good gifts** to your children, how much more will your heavenly Father **give the Holy Spirit** to those who ask Him!* Luke 11:13 NKJ

In Matthew's account of this same passage, Jesus calls the Holy Spirit a good thing and a good gift:

> *If you then, being evil, know how to give **good gifts**
> to your children, how much more will your Father who
> is in heaven give **good things** to those who ask Him!*
> Matthew 7:11 NKJ

Notice how God calls the Holy Spirit a good gift in Luke's gospel and a good thing in Matthew's gospel. The gift of the Holy Spirit is a good gift from God (The Promise of the Father) and a good thing!

The Holy Spirit came on the day of Pentecost as recorded in Acts 2 and has never left:

> *When the Day of Pentecost had fully come, they were all
> with one accord in one place. And suddenly there came a
> sound from heaven, as of a rushing mighty wind, and it
> filled the whole house where they were sitting. Then there
> appeared to them divided tongues, as of fire, and one sat
> upon each of them. And they were all **filled with the
> Holy Spirit** and began to speak with other tongues, as
> the Spirit gave them utterance.* Acts 2:1-4 NKJ

Later in this same chapter, Peter explains who this baptism is for and how long it would last:

> *Then Peter said to them, "Repent, and let every one of you
> be baptized in the name of Jesus Christ for the remission*

*of sins; and you shall receive the **gift** of the Holy Spirit.
For the promise is to you and your children, and to all
who are afar off, as many as the Lord our God will call."*
Acts 2:38-39 NKJ

The gift of the Holy Spirit is the promise of the Father. Jesus
prepared His disciples to receive this promise: *"And you are witnesses
of these things, Behold, I send the **Promise** of My Father upon you:
but tarry in the city of Jerusalem until you are endued with power
from on high."* (Luke 24:48-49 NKJ). That is exactly what they did.
They went to Jerusalem and tarried in an upper room until the Holy
Spirit came. God sent the promise, and they were all filled and began
to speak with other tongues as the Spirit gave them utterance (Acts
2:4).

Peter taught the people to repent of their sins and be baptized by
the Spirit into the family of God (the first baptism). Then they
were water baptized in Jesus' name (the second baptism). Once they
believed, they were able to receive the gift and the "Promise of the
Father" or the Holy Spirit (the third baptism). Peter also assured
them that the gift of the Holy Spirit was for them, their children, and
those afar off (us), to even as many as the Lord calls (each generation).

Receiving the Gift of the Holy Spirit

The Baptism of the Holy Spirit is a gift, and like all gifts must be received. Just like we received the gift of eternal life (Jesus), we now receive the gift of the Holy Spirit (from Jesus).

And it happened, while Apollos was at Corinth, that Paul, having passed through the upper regions, came to Ephesus. And finding some disciples he said to them "Did you receive the Holy Spirit when you believed?" So, they said to him, "We have not so much as heard whether there is a Holy Spirit." And he said to them, "Into what then were you baptized?" So, they said, "Into John's baptism." Then Paul said, "John indeed baptized with a baptism of repentance, saying to the people that they should believe on Him who would come after him, that is, on Christ Jesus." When they heard this, they were baptized in the name of the Lord Jesus. And when Paul had laid hands on them, the Holy Spirit came upon them, and they spoke with tongues and prophesied. Acts 19:1-6 NKJ

Here we find the Apostle Paul ministering to John's disciples and teaching them how to go forward in their commitment to Christ. While they did believe in Jesus, they had not been baptized nor had heard of the gift of the Holy Spirit. After listening to Paul, they were water baptized in Jesus' name, and then received the gift of the Holy Spirit and spoke with other tongues and prophesied.

Speaking in other tongues is where so many get tripped up. Lots of questions come up and need to be addressed. "Can I be filled and not speak in tongues?" "What is the purpose of tongues?" "Is this for today?" "Didn't this die and pass away with the last Apostle?" On and on it goes with what people have heard versus what God's word says. Everyone has an opinion on this subject, including lost people. Jesus called the gift of the Holy Spirit a good gift. I have dedicated an entire chapter to the subject of speaking in other tongues.

Many have not been taught the difference between the gift of the Holy Spirit and the gift of tongues. The gift of the Holy Spirit is for all believers who ask and believe they receive. The gift of tongues is one of the nine spiritual gifts recorded in 1 Corinthians 12. What is the difference? The gift of the Holy Spirit, with the evidence of speaking with other tongues, is the infilling of the Holy Spirit into your inner man. Tongues is a prayer language given at the time of infilling that when spoken, magnifies God. Those who heard the tongues of those filled with the Spirit on the day of Pentecost, heard them speak in their native language *the wonderful works of God* (Acts 2:11). Those filled were speaking in a tongue that was not known to them but was recognized by those around them. The unknown tongue to the speaker was known by the hearers in the crowd. They heard them speak and declare the wonderful works of God in their own native tongue.

Peter, who spoke in tongues, stood up later with the eleven and said to the crowd, *"Men of Judea and all who dwell in Jerusalem, let this be known to you and heed my words."* (Acts 2:14 NKJ). Peter explained to the crowd in a commonly known language what was happening around them. This unknown tongue was their spirit speaking to God, thanking Him. When we speak in an unknown tongue it is our spirit speaking to God (1 Corinthians 14:2).

The nine gifts of the Spirit are listed in 1 Corinthians 12. They are distributed throughout the body of Christ, and we do not all have the same gifts or all the gifts individually:

> *But the manifestation of the Spirit is given to each one*
> *for the profit of all: for **to one** is given the word of*
> *wisdom through the Spirit, **to another** the word of*
> *knowledge through the same Spirit, **to another** faith by*
> *the same Spirit, **to another** gifts of healings by the same*
> *Spirit, **to another** the working of miracles, **to another***
> *prophecy, **to another** discerning of spirits, **to another***
> *different kinds of tongues, **to another** the interpretation*
> *of tongues. But one and the same Spirit works all these*
> *things, distributing to each one individually as He wills.*
> 1 Corinthians 12:7-11 NKJ

Scripture reveals these gifts are distributed among us as the Spirit wills. He says to one is given...to another is given and so on. All these gifts are for ministering to the body of Christ. The gift of tongues is one of these nine and not everyone has this gift. This gift needs the gift of interpretation of tongues to work in conjunction with it. The gift of tongues is God speaking to US. We need the interpretation to know what God is saying. On the other hand, the gift of the Holy Spirit and speaking with other tongues is us speaking to God: *"For he who speaks in a tongue does not speak to men **but to God**, for no one understands him; however, in the spirit he speaks mysteries."* (1 Corinthians 14:2 NKJ). I will go into detail in the next chapter concerning speaking in tongues.

- Gift of the Holy Spirit – You speak mysteries to God in the Spirit

- Gift of Tongues – God speaking to us in the assembly must be interpreted.

"Do all have the gifts of healings?" (1 Corinthians 12:30). The answer is no. However, all can lay hands on the sick and pray for healing, but all do not have this gift. *"Do all speak with tongues?"* (1 Corinthians 12:30). The answer is no. All do not have this gift; however, all can receive the gift of the Holy Spirit and pray in tongues.

Chapter 9

SPEAKING WITH OTHER TONGUES

*And they were all filled with the Holy Spirit and began to speak with **other tongues**, as the Spirit gave them utterance.*

Acts 2:4 NKJ

With the gift of the Holy Spirit comes an utterance with other tongues, what is often called a prayer language. On the day of Pentecost, the people began to speak with other tongues as the Holy Spirit gave them utterance. Just to be clear, the Holy Spirit does not speak with other tongues, rather, we do. We must speak by faith as the Spirit gives us utterance.

I am often asked, "Can I be baptized with the Holy Spirit and not speak in other tongues?" This question reveals a basic misunderstanding of this manifestation of being filled with the Spirit. If we understand praying in other tongues, then why would we not want to? I guess you can buy a car without an engine, but why would you? A house without doors? A bicycle without wheels? Those things tend to come with the purchased items. Tongues, and speaking with other tongues, are part of the total package of the gift of the Holy Spirit. That is the consistent witness of being filled or baptized with the Holy Spirit.

Paul spoke of speaking with other tongues more than all the Corinthian believers:

> *I thank my God **I speak with tongues more than you all**; yet in the Church I would rather speak five words with my understanding, that I may teach others also, than ten thousand words in a tongue.* 1 Corinthians 14:18 NKJ

PURPOSE OF SPEAKING IN TONGUES

In 1 Corinthians 14, Paul explains what happened when he spoke in other tongues. I am only going to highlight these passages because the purpose of speaking in other tongues is a book in and of itself. This is one of those subjects that everyone has an opinion on. Even lost people usually have something to say about speaking with other tongues. I just want to show you what the Scriptures say regarding this topic. What the Bible says is God's opinion and that is the one that really matters.

Paul is bringing order, and divine structure to our public gatherings and how things should work regarding the gifts and order of services. Speaking in other tongues in public meetings was an issue, and Paul was willing to address their misunderstandings. In addressing certain issues, he explains the purpose of speaking in other tongues. Paul compares speaking in tongues (the unknown language of the spirit) to prophecy; (a known language of the Spirit).

> *Pursue love, and desire spiritual gifts, but especially that you may prophesy. For he who speaks in a tongue does **not speak to men but to God**, for no one understands him; however, **in the spirit he speaks mysteries**.* I Corinthians 14:1-2 NKJ

According to Paul:

1. When we prophesy, we speak to men in an inspired known tongue. Prophecy is more like God speaking to us. On the other hand, when we speak in other tongues we speak to God, not man. That is why it doesn't matter what it sounds like or what men think. In our public gatherings, we need to hear from God and so prophecy is the greater need.

2. We are speaking mysteries in the spirit. These are things that are hidden from our carnal, unrenewed minds but are spoken directly to God from our spirit.

3. *"But he who prophesies speaks edification and exhortation and comfort to men. He who speaks in a tongue edifies himself, but he who prophesies edifies the church. I wish you all spoke with tongues, but even more that you prophesied; for he who prophesies is greater than he who speaks with tongues, unless indeed he interprets, that the church may receive edification."* (1 Corinthians 14:3-5 NKJ). Prophecy edifies, exhorts, and comforts others and the church. When we speak in an unknown tongue, we edify ourselves. Someone might say, "I want to edify the Church instead of myself." While that sounds noble and virtuous, we cannot edify others if we are not edified. The purpose of us being edified is not selfish, but to edify others. We cannot edify others if we are not edified. These verses put the greater blessing on prophesying—so that is the goal. If we can interpret what we are speaking in the unknown language of the spirit, then that would be equal to prophecy. Speaking in tongues is a means to an end...being edified to edify. *"Even so you, since you are zealous for spiritual gifts, let it be for the edification of the church that you seek to excel."* (1 Corinthians 14:12 NKJ)

4. *"For if I pray in a tongue, **my spirit prays**, but my understanding is unfruitful."* (1 Corinthians 14:14 NKJ). When we pray and speak in tongues, our spirit prays, but our mind or understanding is unfruitful in that we do not know what we are saying. In other words, we are not praying or speaking from our own understanding, but the

mysteries that are in our spirit, in Christ. WOW! Our spirit is bypassing our carnal minds, speaking and praying directly to God. How awesome is that? Most people do not even know they have a spirit. That is the part of us that is born again. The part that is a new creation (2 Corinthians 5:17). The part of us that is righteous and truly holy. (Romans 5:19 / 2 Corinthians 5:21 / Ephesians 4:24)

5. *"What is the conclusion then? I will pray with the spirit, and I will also pray with the understanding. I will sing with the spirit, and I will also sing with the understanding."* (1 Corinthians 14:15 NKJ). Just like we can pray with our spirit and our understanding, we can sing with both as well. This verse answers that serious question that many ask, "Can I turn it off and on?" Just like we pray with our understanding (our known language) and God partners with us when we pray, so it is when we pray in an unknown language (tongues). God is not taking over your tongue and making us speak. We can choose to speak in tongues or not. "I **will** pray with the spirit, and I will also pray with the understanding." These are both acts of our free will (choice). Acts 2:4 says, *"and **they** were all filled with the Holy Spirit and began to **speak** with other tongues, as the **Spirit gave them utterance.**"* As we choose to open our mouths and speak, the Spirit gives us the ability to do so in an unknown language. The Holy Spirit is not speaking, we are. The Holy Spirit provides the utterance, by choice and

faith we must do the speaking. We are in control of praying in the spirit as we are when we pray in our known language. God does not make us speak in tongues, He provides the utterance to speak, and we speak in faith.

6. *"Otherwise, if you **bless with the spirit**, how will he who occupies the place of the uninformed say "amen" at your **giving of thanks**, since he does not understand what you say?"* (1 Corinthians 14:16 NKJ). Remember, when we speak in tongues we are speaking to God, not men (vs. 1-2). Therefore, we are giving thanks to God, not men. Our spirit is never depressed, discouraged, or lacking in faith, peace, or joy. It is our souls (minds) that are subject to these things. Our spirit knows nothing but joy and peace. That is the part of us that is speaking to God. It is not only refreshing and edifying to us, but we're also sure God is blessed. **And yes, we can and do bless the Lord.**

7. (Vs. 16) When we pray in the Spirit, we are blessing God from our spirit man. Remember that our spirit is righteous and truly holy, complete in Christ. That part of us is blessed and very thankful to God.

8. *"For you indeed **give thanks well**..."* (1 Corinthians 14:17 NKJ). Speaking in tongues is a great way to give thanks to the Lord and do it well.

9. *"I thank my God I speak with tongues more than you all;*

yet in the church I would rather speak five words with my understanding, that I may teach others also, than ten thousand words in a tongue. "(1 Corinthians 14:18-19 NKJ) Praying in other tongues is to minister to the Lord from our spirit man, and then from there, to prophecy and teach. We are to share in a known tongue in the assembly to edify others.

Jude sums it up in his own way:

> *But you, beloved, **building yourselves up** on your most holy faith, **praying in the Holy Spirit**, keep yourselves in the love of God, looking for the mercy of our Lord Jesus Christ unto eternal life.* Jude 1:20-21 NKJ

We build ourselves up on our most holy faith when we pray in the Holy Spirit so we can build others up. We also are keeping ourselves in the love of God as we watch for God's mercy in this newfound life of the Spirit. Ask Jesus to baptize you with the Holy Spirit and believe you will receive when you ask. Find a believer filled with the spirit to pray with you or have some spirit-filled believers lay hands on you to receive this gift from God. When you understand the purpose of speaking with other tongues or praying in the Holy Spirit, you then can understand 1 Corinthians 14:39-40 (KJV): *Wherefore brethren, covet to prophesy and **forbid not** to speak with tongues. Let all things be done decently and in order.*

Chapter 10

IDENTITY IN CHRIST

Therefore, if anyone is in Christ, he is a new creation; old things have passed away; behold, all things have become new. Now all things are of God, who has reconciled us to Himself through Jesus Christ, and has given us the ministry of reconciliation...

2 Corinthians 5:17-18 NKJ

I would like to start this chapter by pointing out three important facts regarding our identity:

1. Our identity connects us to our purpose.

2. Identity sets the course for and affects the quality of our lives.

3. Our new identity brings healing and wholeness to our personhood.

As you read this chapter, you will begin to understand each of these points. One of the most important revelations we receive as Christians is understanding our new identity in Christ. To explain this properly, I need to go back to the beginning. At the start of Creation, we were all inside of Adam. The whole human race was identified in Adam. We all come out of and from Adam.

Adam was a representative man who stood on behalf of the human race. He was the Father of the first creation. He was the master copy for the entire human race. He was created righteous and truly holy. He had a perfect relationship and fellowship with God. That was the condition we would have all been born in had Adam not sinned. He would fill the earth with people after his own kind (righteous and truly holy). We would have been born in that same condition.

We were inside Adam like a child is in their mother. Where the mother goes, the child goes. I live in Oklahoma and if my child is born in Oklahoma, they will be called an Okie. But if my wife and I move to Texas, the child will be called a Texan. What the child is called is not determined by the child, but by the parent. Adam was righteous and had he not sinned we would have been born into that righteousness. However, he moved from the state of righteousness to the state of unrighteousness. So now, by no fault of our own, we were born in the state of unrighteousness in need of a savior. We were "IN ADAM" and identified in him.

Satan knew that if he could steal Adam's identity as God's prized creation, he could rob all of us of ours as well. So, he devised a scheme to deceive Adam, thereby causing Adam's identity to become skewed. Rather than Adam finding his identity in simple faith obedience to God, his disobedience in sin damaged his identity and relationship with God. He went from a state or condition of righteousness to one of sin. Eating the forbidden tree in disobedience to God (Genesis 3) brought about death, sickness, poverty, insecurity, and many other symptoms of darkness. Adam's identity was no longer focused on God and His righteousness but now was focused on sin and self. He went from being dominated by God, the Holy Spirit, and His Word, to being dominated by sin, Satan, and his flesh. He was now being influenced by his five physical senses and his own determined philosophies, living in a fallen, broken identity. It is the same with us. Before we are saved, we are what the Bible describes as being "in Adam" and in Adam, our identity is bound by sin, death, sickness, and poverty. All our negative attitudes and actions are simply the overflow of that stolen, broken identity and will create disasters in our lives.

When we are born again, our identity changes from a person of sin to one of righteousness in Christ. Because of this, we can identify with what Christ says to be true about each of us. We are no longer who we were in Adam but are now a new creation in Christ. When we are saved, we are united to Christ. By faith in Him, we are a part of the family of God. In Christ, we are made righteous, healed by His stripes, have eternal life, and are abundantly blessed. Why is understanding what we have in Christ so important? Because it is the foundation for all the blessings and promises God has made in the new covenant.

When we are born again, we are made completely new in our spirit man. Our soul (mind will and emotions) is now in the process of becoming new as we renew our minds to God's word. Our bodies are not changed, or become new, but are saved by hope (future tense) at the resurrection. That happens when Jesus returns in all His glory.

Continuing in 2 Corinthians 5:18, *"and all things are of God..."* is referring to our spirit man. All things are not of God in our carnal, unrenewed minds. All things are not new in our bodies. It is our born-again spirit that all things are new, and now of God. We are part of a new family, a new Kingdom, and we have a new inheritance in Christ. Our new life in Christ is now a journey and adventure into discovering all the promises of God. Each new day is one of excitement for all the NEW things God has promised and prepared for all those who are now IN CHRIST. We will spend a lifetime on this adventure of discovering all the "newness" that God has for us.

One of the first and foremost discoveries is our new identity. Who we are in Christ and the new us as a Christian. We are no longer who we were in Adam but are now a new creation in Christ. "In Adam" refers to our old condition before being saved. "In Christ" refers to our new condition as a Christian. We all were inside of Adam and came from him as a part of the family of man. In Adam is our old identity bound by sin, death, sickness, and poverty. When we are saved, we become a part of Jesus and, by faith in Him, are a part of the family of God. God only sees two families, the family of God or the "Adam's family". Do you remember the "Addams family" that was a TV series years ago? They were the strange ones yet thought everyone else was strange. Those still in Adam in the world think we are the strange ones. We are all in one family or the other. In Christ, we are made righteous, healed by His stripes, have eternal life, and are abundantly blessed. This new identity is the foundation for all the blessings and promises God has made in the new covenant.

Many elements contribute to and shape our identity. How we identify ourselves affects our quality of life. Because Satan understands this, he desires to damage our identity in any way he can. Most people live their lives with a broken identity, a false identity, or even a stolen identity. All our actions come out of our identity. In other words, who we are, or even believe ourselves to be, affects both our attitude and actions. When we put our identity squarely in Christ it changes both.

Look at 2 Corinthians 5:17 in different translations:

> *"This means that anyone who belongs to Christ has become a new person. The old life is gone; a new life has begun!"* (NLT)

> *"...anyone united with the Messiah gets a fresh start, is created new. "*(MSG)

> *"Now, if anyone is enfolded into Christ, he has become an entirely new person, all that is related to the old order has vanished."* (TPT)

> *"Therefore if any person is [ingrafted] in Christ (the Messiah) he is a new creation (a new creature altogether); the old (previous moral and spiritual condition) has passed away. Behold, the fresh and new has come!"* (AMPC)

We are no longer the person we used to be "in Adam" but are now a new person "in Christ." This is all a fact in your spirit man. We are part of a new family, a new Kingdom, and we have a new inheritance. Each new day is one of excitement for all the NEW things God has promised and prepared for all those who are now IN CHRIST. We will spend a lifetime on this adventure of discovering all the "newness" that God has for us.

Our identity in Christ is how God originally intended us to be before sin came into the world. When we are born again, our new identity is created in the image of Christ: – *"and have put on the **new man** who is renewed in knowledge according to the **image of Him** who created him,"* (Colossians 3:10 NKJ). It is one spirit with the Lord: – *"But he who is **joined to the Lord** is one spirit with Him."* (1 Corinthians 6:17 NKJ). Sin has blitzed and blighted God's image in man and made us all less than God intended for us to be (Genesis 1:26-29). Our new identity is bringing us back to what God intended in the creation and willed for humanity.

In Romans 5:12-19 Paul compares the life of Adam and Jesus and how it affects all of us. Adam's disobedience to God had a profound effect on all of us. However, that is also true of Jesus and His obedience. Adam's disobedience made us all sinners, but Jesus' obedience at the cross has made us righteous. – *"...as by one man's* (Adam) *disobedience many were **made sinners**, so also by one Man's obedience many will be **made righteous**."* (Romans 5:19 NKJ). *"For He (God) hath made him (Jesus) to be sin for us (you), who knew no sin; that we might be **made the righteousness of God** in him."* (2 Corinthians 5:21 KJV). Yes, it is true, we were all made sinners by another man's sin, but we were also made righteous by another man's holiness. We were born into sin (1st birth), and we must be born out of sin into righteousness (2nd birth). Simply put, Adam got us into sin, and Jesus got us out.

Think of how radical those two concepts are and how radical our new identity is now in Christ. Our understanding of this new identity changes everything, and I truly mean EVERYTHING! If we believe we are still an "old sinner saved by grace," then the brokenness of sin is not healed. But what if we begin to believe that, because we are now in Christ, we are "the righteousness of God saved by grace"? Now our new identity heals the brokenness of sin and that can and will affect all areas of our lives. Understanding our righteousness in Christ sets us free from condemnation, guilt, and shame. Righteousness by faith is more than a doctrinal truth, it is a new creation reality!

> ***Awake to righteousness***, *and do not sin; for some do*
> *not have the knowledge of God. I speak this to your shame.*
> 1 Corinthians 15:34 NKJ

All our actions are a result of who we believe ourselves to be. Discovering who we are in Christ will affect all our choices. Cows "moo" because they are cows. Cats "meow" because they are cats. Dogs "bark" because they are dogs. What they do is a result of who and what they are. By that same token, we do not do works of righteousness to become righteous, instead, we are righteous right now in Christ.

Out of our new righteous condition, we do acts of righteousness and good works. Jesus describes us as *"the light of the world."* Our new identity in Christ has made us a light and as a light, we shine in good works. We are the *"salt of the earth,"* because of who we are in our born-again spirit. We make a difference as salt and light in a dark world.

It is a shame that Christians do not have the knowledge of being made righteous in God's eyes by faith. As a new believer, it is vital to discover who we are now in Christ. How do we do that? Well, for one thing, we do not discover our new identity or who we are based on our five senses (sight, smell, hearing, taste, or feeling). We do not use our emotions to tell us who we are either because we cannot always see or feel our born-again spirit. This is where God's word is vital. God's word is spirit and reveals what is spirit:

*"It is the Spirit who gives life; the flesh profits nothing. The **words** that I speak to you are **spirit**, and they are life."* John 6:63 NKJ

"God is Spirit, and those who worship Him must worship in spirit and truth." John 4:24 NKJ

We cannot contact God or connect with Him through our souls or bodies. However, all of us know God by Spirit (Holy Spirit) and truth (His word). Our new identity is rooted and grounded in Christ Who is united to our spirit. Understanding this truth is directly connected to our maturity. Paul declares this mystery and connection – *"...the mystery which has been hidden from ages and from generations, but now has been revealed to His saints, to them God willed to make known what are the riches of the glory of this mystery among the Gentiles..."* (Colossians 1:26-27 NKJ).

Notice there is a mystery (divine secret hidden in God) that has been hidden that is now revealed to God's saints. There are great riches connected to this mystery. What is the mystery? *"Which is Christ in you, the hope of glory."* Our new identity in Christ is the mystery and now the hope of all glory. The next statement is profound: - *"Him we preach, warning every man and **teaching** every man in all wisdom, that we may present every man perfect (mature) in Christ Jesus."* (Colossians 1:28 NKJ). This is what produces maturity in our lives. When we see who we are in Christ progressively, we go from convert to disciple. The Apostle Paul labored and taught this revelation to bring about supernatural change in us and the church. God's word on who we are in Christ is like a mirror of the Spirit, revealing this rich mystery of Christ in you, the hope of glory.

Chapter 11

DISCOVERING OUR IDENTITY

Sanctify them by Your truth. Your word is truth:

John 17:17 NKJ

Then Jesus said to those Jews who believed Him, "If you abide in My word, you are My disciples indeed. And you shall know the truth, and the truth shall make you free. John 8:31-32

NKJ

The truth of who we are in Christ is revealed in the scriptures. That truth brings freedom. God reveals Himself by revelation and in His Scriptures. He also reveals to us who we are in the same way.

Just like a physical mirror connects us to our body and our intellect connects us to our emotions and souls, God's word is a mirror of the Spirit realm. What God says about us in Scripture is true in our spirit man. God's word reveals and declares our new life in Christ.

DUANE SHERIFF

As our minds are renewed by His Word, our attitudes and actions will change, and our lives will be transformed.

> *"And do not be **conformed** to this world, but be **transformed** by the **renewing of your mind**, that you may prove what is that good and acceptable and perfect will of God."* Romans 12:2 NKJ

> *"that you put off, concerning your former conduct, the old man which grows corrupt according to the deceitful lusts, and **be renewed in the spirit of your mind**, and that you put on the new man which was created according to God, in true righteousness and holiness."* Ephesians 4:22-24 NKJ

> *"and have put on the new man who is renewed in knowledge according to the **image of Him** who created him,"* Colossians 3:10 NKJ

You have been made a new person in your spirit. Now, you must put on your new identity through mind renewal. As your mind is renewed to who you are on the inside, you are transformed on the outside. The word "transformed" in the original Greek language is "metamorphoo" (Strongs G3339). The English word metamorphosis comes from this word. Metamorphosis is the radical change of the structure of an animal by supernatural means. A caterpillar becomes a butterfly. A tadpole becomes a bullfrog. Those are both radical changes. They both came from the inside out. The caterpillar was a butterfly on the inside but had to go through a metamorphosis to experience on the outside who and what it was meant to be. It is the same for the tadpole.

Likewise, you are a new creation in your spirit and as your minds are renewed to who and what you are in Christ, your life will experience outwardly what is already a reality inwardly. Your born-again spirit is perfect, just, and made righteous. It is your carnal, unrenewed mind that needs changed and renewed to God's word. Your mind has been programmed with death, doubt, lack, poverty, sickness, disease, and defeat. God wants you to displace those negative, worldly thoughts with His thoughts of life, faith, abundance, prosperity, healing, wholeness, and victory. Discovering your new identity in Christ is powerful. God has not called you to develop a high self-esteem, but rather a high Christ-esteem. Seeing Christ in yourself can deliver you from inferiorities, complexes, and negative images of yourself.

Because I understand that beginning this discovery of your new identity can be overwhelming, I recommend reading the New Testament at first. Everything it declares you to "be" is true in your spirit man. Read the New Testament repeatedly and it will reveal this new condition your spirit enjoys. The Holy Spirit brings revelation to your mind of the new creation realities.

Above everything else, believe who God says you are in Christ, especially more than how you look or feel on the outside. Remember, your body and unrenewed mind bear the image of the old you. Your spirit bears the image of Christ. Believe what God says and agree with Him as a confession of faith. Everything God says you are in Christ is true, regardless of anything or anyone else. God says you are righteous in Him, so you need to agree in faith and say what God says. There may be times that you are not acting or feeling righteous in your body or mind; however, in God's eyes, your spirit man in Christ is righteous. Once your mind is renewed to who you are in Christ, your attitudes and actions will begin to reflect that.

As you read the New Testament, take heed to all the prepositional phrases that connect us to Christ: "in Christ," "with Christ," "through Christ," "together with Christ," "in Him," "with Him," "through Him." All these phrases are declaring our new identity. They are describing our new condition and position in Christ.

SOME EXAMPLES

> "...for *in Him* we live and move and have our being, as also some of your own poets have said, '*For we are also His offspring*'." Acts 17:28 NKJ

Our new life is from Him now. We are living and moving from this new condition in Christ. We are a new person in Him. Notice we are His very offspring, now born of God. That is an awesome identity!

> *"Therefore if anyone is **in Christ**, he is a new creation..."*
> 2 Corinthians 5:17 NKJ

> *"Yet in all these things we are more than conquerors **through Him** Who loves us.* Romans 8:37 NKJ

All these identity scriptures are a reality in your spirit. They are who God declares you to be and as you mix faith with these blessings of grace, your life is changed.

Now I pray that you become a disciple of our Lord Jesus Christ. This new life in Christ is an exciting journey as you walk with the Lord in relationship and fellowship.

Understanding our new life in Christ and Christ living in us, is the road to maturity and victory in this life. Enjoy learning and experiencing Him daily as you seek first God's kingdom!

ABOUT THE AUTHOR

Duane Sheriff is in author, international speaker and the Founding Pastor and Senior Elder of Victory Life Church, a multi-campus church which is headquartered in Durant, OK. Duane travels the world speaking at conferences, and churches, and is a frequent teacher at Charis Bible College. He has a passion to help people discover their identity in Christ and help them be transformed through the Word of God. His first book, *Identity Theft*, was released in 2017. Since then he has authored several more books including: *Our Union with Christ, Better Together,* and *Counterculture.* He also has a television ministry that broadcasts on various stations. Pastor Duane and his wife, Sue have been married since 1980 and together have four children and eleven grandchildren.

For free teachings by Pastor Duane visit his website at **www.pastorduane.com**

ADDITIONAL RESOURCES

If you would like more information about your new identity in Christ, I have two books that cover this topic in detail and practical application – "Identity Theft" and "Our Union with Christ." The first book, "Identity Theft" covers how sin and Satan have robbed us of our identity, creating disasters in our lives. All our negative attitudes and actions are simply the overflow of a broken or stolen identity. The first thing God does in our life at the new birth is healing our identity. He makes us a new creation to reverse these negative attitudes and actions. Out of this new creation flows thankful attitudes and God's blessing in seeing who we now are in Christ.

In my second book, "Our Union with Christ," I explore the reality of being joined to the Lord in spirit like a husband and wife are in marriage. We become one flesh in holy matrimony with our spouse. We become one spirit with Jesus at the new birth. We are "the bride of Christ" and Jesus is the bridegroom. Our union is described in scripture to be like a husband and wife in marriage. Jesus is our husband, and we are His beloved bride. He is the best husband ever, abounding toward us in grace and love.

We are to be the submissive loving wife responding in faith. His love for us is intense and passionate. Our commitment and loyalty to Him should be unprecedented. I describe how He loves us and how it relates to a marriage relationship.

I also have free audio teachings that cover these subjects and others in more detail. Please avail yourself of these materials at *pastorduane.com*.

Enjoy your new life in Christ and purpose in your heart to become a disciple, not just a convert.

Made in the USA
Columbia, SC
16 April 2024